Her Good Nights

Author Bridgett Brown-Burkes and Co-Author Dontasia Burkes

Illustrated By Kendal Williams

Dontasia is playing in her
room happy and smiling,
minding her own business.
As she is playing, she hears
the shower turn on.

She instantly runs out
the room to check.

Time to Shower!!

(She sees the shower has been turned on.
She began to run through the house as
far away as possible from the bathroom.)

"Dontasia!" called Mom.

"She's coming!" said Dontasia.

"Time to take a shower. Let's go to the bathroom," instructed Daddy.

"No take a shower! No Bathroom!" pouted Dontasia

"Yes, bathroom!" said her mother. (Her mother is chasing her continuously around the house, through the rooms and the kitchen. Dontasia is sliding on the floor and climbing across the couches. She is breathing hard, laughing, and excited to play. Her parents can't catch her.)

Her mom stopped and said, "I'm tired, Toot! Now, it is time to shower!" Her mom called Dontasia by her nickname.

(Mom begins to walk away from Toot and heads to the bathroom. Dontasia call for her mom.)

"Hey, let's go! Come here!" demanded Toot.

(Mom comes and Dontasia flies away again.
 Mom walks away. Dontasia begins to call for her dad now.)

"Daddy, where are you? Come here!" she shouted.

(Mom and Dad both come this time and Dontasia runs again. This time she is exhausted and not moving so fast. Dad finally catches her.)

"Shirt off," said Dontasia.

"Yes, take your shirt off," agreed her mom.

(She holds Dontasia hand, so she doesn't run off again.)

(Finally, 20 minutes has passed and Dontasia is in the shower. She is singing a variety of tunes. She loves to sing in the shower.)

(Mom helps her out.)

"Time to get out & lotion up," said mom.

(Dontasia reaches out her hand to get some lotion to put on her legs. Next, she puts on her pajamas. Now she is already for bed, but she is definitely not ready to go to sleep.)

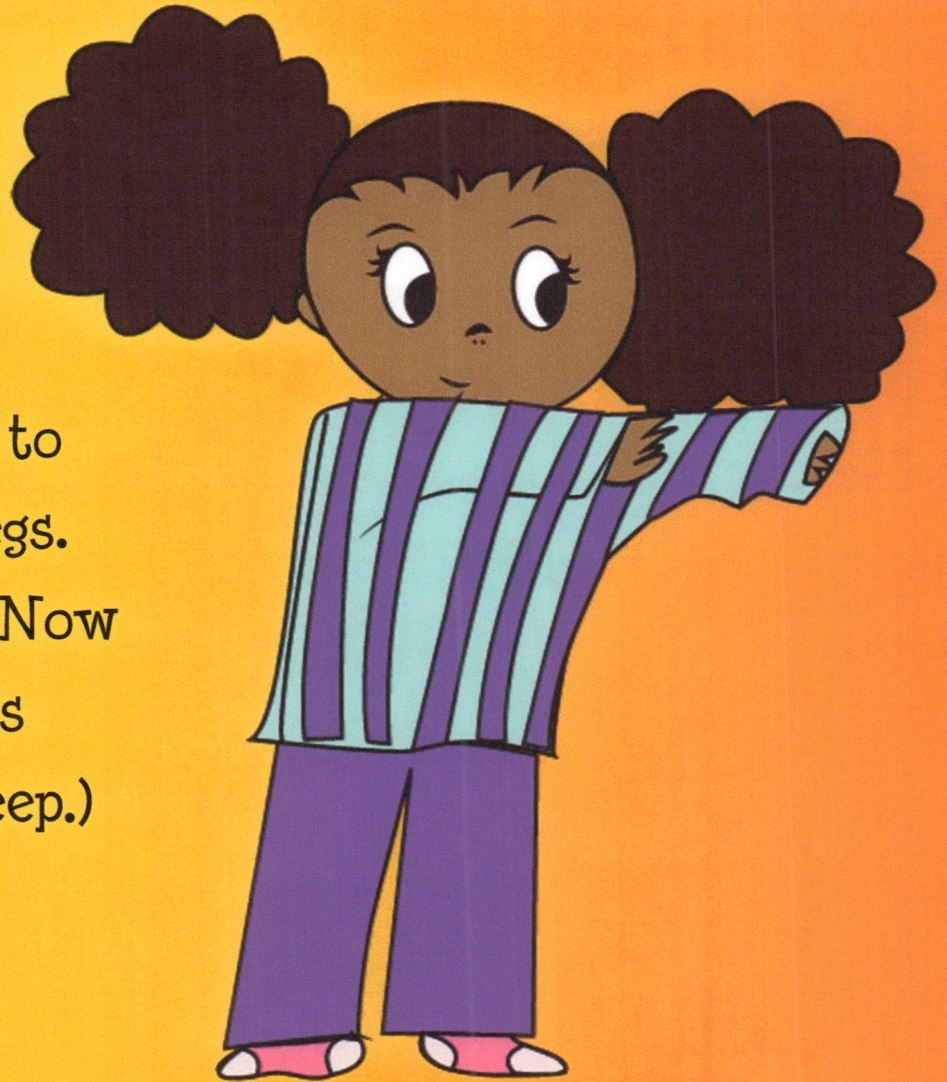

Dontasia did everything she could to avoid going to sleep. She took all of her teddy bears to her parent's room and threw them in the bed. With her parents lying in a bed full of teddy bears, Dontasia squeezed herself in the bed, too.

She noticed her sticker book and began to place stickers on her dad.

Dontasia shouted, "Time to clean up!"

One-by-one, she grabbed each teddy bear and threw them in an empty laundry basket with smiles and laughter.

She cleaned up the bears and the laughter stopped. She yelled, "Wait, orange...orange!"

"Where is your cup, Dontasia?" she asked her mom.

"It's over there! It's over there!" Dontasia shouted.

"Go get it," her mother stated.

Dontasia yelled again, "It's over there!"

Dad grabbed the cup. Her mother grabbed the juice, hoping Dontasia would fall asleep. Holding her cup, she fell back in bed, hummed a rhythmic tune, and clapped her hands.

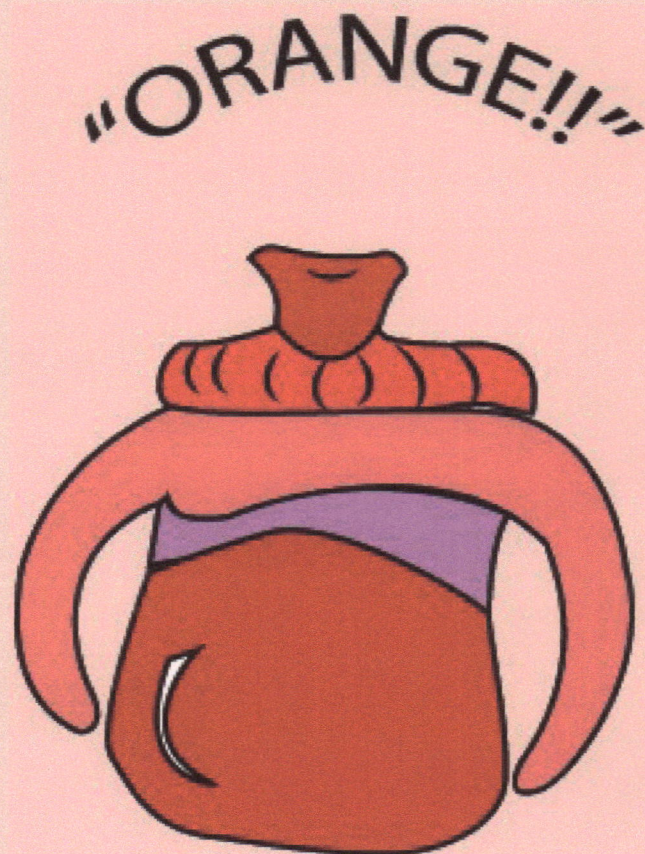

"ORANGE!!"

All of a sudden, she popped up and ran to the living room looking for her Legos. She grabbed them all, making several trips back-and-forth from her room to the dining room. Sitting at the dining room table, Dontasia continued to sip her cup as she created a beautiful image. After 45 minutes, Dontasia was almost done creating her vision.

"ORANGE!!"

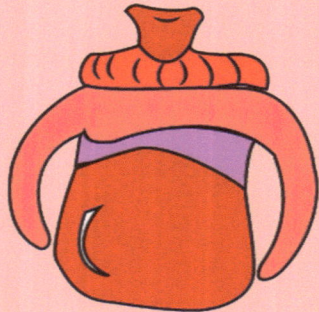

It was after midnight and Dontasia was still up. She headed to the couch and grabbed a throw blanket. Mom and Dad were watching as they anticipated she would fall asleep.

Grabbing the remote, Mom searched for something on television. Immediately, Toot sat up and said, "No, that's not it. Keep going!"

Moving her hand in the direction she wanted her mother to go, she finally said, "Right there!" Toot sat up to watch television as if sleep was not on the agenda.

After 10 minutes she yelled, "Pizza, pizza! I want pizza!" Her dad got up to warm a slice of pizza for her. Her mom looked at Dontasia, barely keeping her eyes open and asked, "Are you not sleepy?"

"No go to sleep. No sleep!" said Dontasia.

Dad gave her the pizza. She sat up with her hand extended, pointing to the Kitchen. "Wash your hands, wash your hands!" she said.

"Do you want a napkin?" Dad asked before grabbing her a napkin.

As she ate, Dontasia started to look very tired. Her eyes were gloomy, and her body started to slouch down on the couch.

After five minutes, she leaned over, still trying to eat her pizza. Her eyes blink...blink...blinked until they finally closed.

Watching her quietly, as she floats away into a deep sleep. The cup fell out of Dontasia's hand hitting the floor. Her mom and dad looked at each other, hoping the sound didn't wake her.

"BLANKET!"

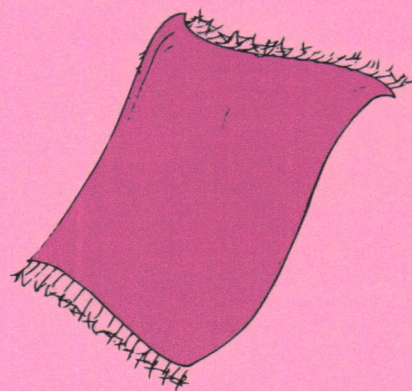

Dontasia moved, but only to get in a comfortable position. She sleepily said, "Blanket, blanket."

Dad covered her up with a blanket. Dontasia looked at him and said, "You sleepy, go to sleep!"

Dad replied, "Yes, go to sleep!" Dontasia turned over to a restful position.

Her mom and dad looked at each other and took a deep breath as they shook their heads laughing.
They watched their little girl fall into a peaceful sleep.

Kissing her good night, Mom said, "I love you! Good night my baby!"

goodnight !

They say all children can learn. And I believe this is true! When I first started working with Dontasia I honestly didn't know where to start. Letters? Sounds? Sight words? She loves puzzles. So we started there. She loves music. We did that too. Using what she loves to help her learn. She learned over 30 words in a couple months.. Yes, All children CAN learn! Autistic children too!

-Brianna Forde

Being toot's sister has taught me so much in life! She taught me not to judge someone by the way they look or by the way they are. She taught me how to handle kids with disabilities without treating them any different from others. I remember taking an early childhood class in middle school just to know extra ways to care for her. Toot made me realize that autistic children are VERY smart; they just have different ways of communicating and understanding. I AM SO PROUD TO BE YOUR BIG SISTER!

-Sister/Mommy Bria

Toot-N-Aussie Foundation

ABOUT US

Toot-N-Aussie Foundation, Inc., was created and founded by the mother of Dontasia (Toot) Burkes. Over the years searching for resources, answers, and help; she realized that she had to do something to help those on the spectrum; as well as, those who are caretakers of those on the spectrum.

OUR MISSION

This foundation is designed to not only offer support and resources but to create a supportive community, that will provide an outlet to help others through the process.

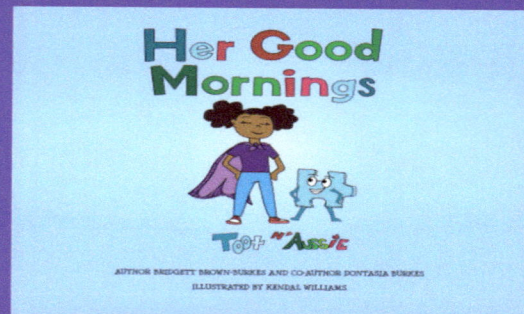

Her Good Mornings

AUTHOR BRIDGETT BROWN-BURKES AND CO-AUTHOR DONTASIA BURKES
ILLUSTRATED BY KENDAL WILLIAMS

Order your copy TODAY!
www.TootNAussie.com

"Together we can"

Giving back through life-changing experiences.

www.ingramcontent.com/pod-product-compliance
Lightning Source LLC
Chambersburg PA
CBHW040405100426

42811CB00017B/1847